Fort Sn
Then and Now:

The World War II Years

Stephen E. Osman

The Friends of Fort Snelling • Saint Paul, Minnesota

For further information please contact the Friends of Fort Snelling:
www.fortsnelling.org

The project was made possible in part by the Arts and Cultural Heritage Fund through the vote of Minnesotans on November 4, 2008. Administered by the Minnesota Historical Society.

About the Photographs
Minnesota Historical Society: Most historic structure images are from the detailed quartermaster volumes, compiled in two sets of two each, ca. 1915–1938 and ca. 1938–1969 (ALPHA, US Army Quartermaster Corps, Fort Snelling Building Records.) The Lawrence Fuller collection of Fort Snelling Research Materials (P2394) provided several images of events and soldiers once published in Minneapolis newspapers. The photograph of recruits in a mess hall line is from the Herbert Schultz Photograph Albums (P2544.) Modern photographs of Historic Fort Snelling buildings formerly numbered 1, 2 and 16 are from the historic site's website.

Edwin M. Nakasone graciously allowed his 1945–46 album to be scanned for this project. Bud arrived at Fort Snelling as a student in the Military Intelligence Service Language School and after a distinguished career retired there as a Colonel, US Army Reserve. Additional images are from Todd Hintz's and from the author's collections. Modern images were taken by Matt Flueger.

The author is grateful to the family of Jacob Klotzbeacher for use of quotations from his manuscript titled "As I Remember It: 1912 to 1992."

ISBN: 978-0-615-46243-1
Printed in the United States of America
Design by Dorie McClelland, www.springbookdesign.com

Contents

Fort Snelling's Last War

WORLD WAR II WAS FORT SNELLING'S LAST WAR. But what was the character of the old post that would host upper Midwestern soldiers counted among the 16 million Americans who served? The Fort was physically a vast complex of offices, warehouses, rail yards, barracks, parade grounds and classrooms sprawled over a 1,500 acre site above the Minnesota and Mississippi Rivers. It was buildings as old as 120 years, solid brick and stone structures on park like green lawns studded with mature elms, and it was hundreds of tar paper and wood frame huts heated with coal stoves. But what was Fort Snelling to the 600,000 men and women who experienced it between 1941 and 1946, most for only a few days or weeks punctuating an active duty that averaged 33 months?

To a regular army officer or enlisted man, the post's historical character made a strong impression. The commander of the Reception Center wrote in 1943:

When I stood at the commandant's house overlooking the junction of the Minnesota and Mississippi rivers and gazed about me, I could hardly fail to realize that I was stationed at a post that was physically older than most of the other forts and posts in the Middle West. How far back in the nation's history this Fort Snelling reached! I could turn and see two buildings that actually dated from the 1820s—the Round Tower, the oldest man-made structure in Minnesota, and the Hexagonal Tower still guarding the actual junction of the two rivers, though its gun ports are laughable now when one considers the size of modern artillery . . . Fort Snelling took its place in the vision of a coast-to-coast United States—a picture, incidentally, that few men were capable of envisioning in the year of our Lord 1820! . . . the men who were responsible for erecting Fort Snelling were not ordinary bureaucrats, but patriots who dared to love their country well enough to think and plan for its future.

To a civilian living in the Twin Cities the fort may not have had such a romantic appeal. Rather it was a social institution and a vital part of the local community. For three generations the famous Third United States Infantry had called the fort home. Polo games attracted thousands as did annual military shows. Summer training camps oriented hundred of local young men to military service. And more recently thousands of GIs flooded the cities while hundreds of civilian volunteers staffed theaters, lounges and service centers both on and off post. To a wide eyed, newly inducted draftee or young volunteer Fort Snelling was the first look at the army. It could be a cold impersonal place with shouting sergeants and overworked clerks, frigid barracks and painful shots, endless waiting in lines and that first taste of home-sickness. And to a Japanese American language student just released from the internment camp where his family would spend the rest of the war, Fort Snelling was more than long hours of study. For these men it was a valued place in a military which desperately needed their help and it was social acceptance on post and in the local community.

Fort Snelling was all these things during World War II, but its preparation for service began years earlier. By December 7, 1941, the post was a far different place than it had been just ten years earlier. As Minnesota's only garrisoned post, Fort Snelling received substantial work projects under the Civilian Conservation Corps and later the Works Progress Administration. When President Roosevelt declared a national emergency in September 1939 work on post facilities was nearing completion with most buildings extensively remodeled. It was in these years that many of the beautiful wooden trim features and ornate porches were removed from the late 19th century structures and replaced with functionally plain concrete. At a cost of nearly two million dollars, the riding stable was converted to a field house, the hospital complex expanded, new sports facilities and barracks constructed, utilities upgraded and quartermaster warehouses expanded. The old round tower was even filled with artifacts as a

Recruits at Reception Center, 1942.

historical museum, soon to close. But on the far edge of the post, in a perhaps ominous development, the old post cemetery was converted to the Fort Snelling National Cemetery.

The 1940 Selective Service Act, intended to augment the armed forces and place them on a war footing, continued this renovation and expansion. The Fort Snelling Reception Station was organized in September as an outgrowth of the old Post Recruit and Casual Detachment. Prior to this time individual units had recruited and trained new members. Housed in the old World War I training camp, the Reception Station soon outgrew these quarters and nearly froze out its recruits in the 1940 Armistice Day Blizzard. The old non-insulated buildings of the so called *Turkey Farm* gave way to a complex which would total over three hundred structures by 1943. This outlaying part of the fort, so familiar to both new recruits and returning veterans of World War II, was located on what is now International Airport property and just across from the still standing Fort Snelling Officers' Club.

The old regular army units at the fort were also changing as war approached. The Third Infantry provided cadre for training new units, as it had trained citizen soldiers in the 1920s and 1930s. Battery F of the 14th Field Artillery lost its superbly trained horses to a stable fire in 1939, and was reassigned as a mechanized unit. And the old 7th Tank Company, a part of the post since 1919, was redesignated as infantry and assigned to a new station. But Fort Snelling's history already stretched back well over 100 years. The Minnesota Historical Society concentrates its interpretive effort on 19th century Fort Snelling when Colonel Snelling's Fifth Infantry had completed an impressive and

Tarpaper 'hutments' at the so called Turkey Farm.

enduring monument of stone and timber hundreds of miles beyond the fringe of the frontier. Their mission was to support the civilian operated United States Indian Agency in promoting and protecting the American fur trade and to enforce a permanent peace in the region by control of the Dakota and Ojibwa peoples. As the Treaties of 1837, 1851 and others moved the Indians off their lands and settlers flooded in there was no longer need for a strong local military presence. The entire government reservation, encompassing most of Minneapolis and part of St. Paul was sold in a questionable land deal in 1858 and the fort closed. The Civil War reopened the post in 1861 as a training ground for Minnesota volunteers and coincidentally confirmed sale of the reservation.

Businessman Franklin Steele eventually traded all but 1,500 acres of
the much reduced post for his wartime rental charges to the army. Fort
Snelling stagnated for a few years while the Civil War temporary and
Colonel Snelling's now antiquated buildings deteriorated.

In 1878, the Department of Dakota changed all that. With the
Custer massacre and continuing Indian troubles, Congress spent over
$100,000 on Fort Snelling. Thirty new buildings were put up while

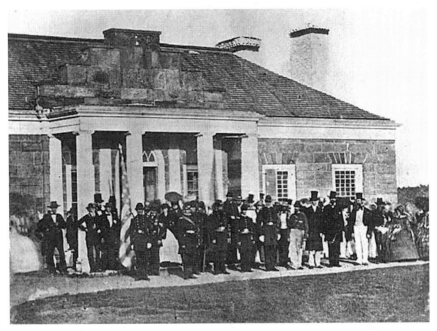

Officers and men of the new First Minnesota Regiment, 1861.

most of the original fort was pulled down and its stones recycled.
Fort Snelling was now headquarters and supply depot for a score of
active smaller posts to the west. Construction continued to the Spanish American War then surged again in 1901 to 1905 when almost 2
million dollars went into the post. As early as 1895, post commander
General Mason had called in vain for preservation: *If the people of
Minnesota would preserve Old Fort Snelling for coming generations,
they should make haste; for sooner or later the buildings so dear to every
Minnesotan will be torn down to make room for needed improvements.*

The popular air conditioned Post Theater.

In the War Department, there is neither romance nor sympathy . . . a museum in the old fort, restored to its former state, would give us a place unique in its character. There would be nothing like it in the United States. General Mason's call went unanswered for another 70 years.

American entry into World War I in 1917 taxed existing post facilities to the limit. The massive brick barracks became a training school for junior officers while the post hospital was designated U.S. General Hospital Number 29 to treat wounded veterans needing rehabilitation. New recruits were housed in the Cantonment, a city of several hundred temporary structures west of the main post. Between the two World Wars the cantonment was summer home to tens of thousands of cadets participating in Reserve Officer Training Corps programs and in Citizen Military Training Camps designed for high school youth. The critical need for this military training was increasingly apparent as war neared: by the late 1930s, twelve foreign powers had military establishments totaling from one to six million trained soldiers, compared to a tiny and ill equipped U.S. regular army of 178,000 men.

Despite the slow move toward war, Fort Snelling was a pleasant post for a soldier during the 1920s and 1930s. The Third Infantry, known

Trick Horse Whiskey performs during the 1920s.

as *The Old Guard*, had called it home since 1888 when they replaced the African American 25th Infantry. The local community considered the Third Infantry as its own. Many local boys enlisted at the fort while their sisters married into the unit. With the largest military game preserve in the nation, a fine golf course, sports facilities, good quarters and easy duty, it was easy to understand why Fort Snelling was known as *The Country Club of the Army*. Citizens flocked to the fort's parade ground or field house to watch polo games and the antics of the trick horse whiskey. Each fall they were treated to the spectacle of a recreated World War I battle. But all of this came to an abrupt end on December 7, 1941.

The most common experience at Fort Snelling during the next five years was that of the *casual*: the recruit, the draftee or the returning veteran who was processed through Reception Station or Separation Point. For a new recruit military service began with a physical examination, often indifferently done by a local doctor working under contract. After a couple of weeks to get his civilian affairs in order, the recruit would be on his way by bus or train to Fort Snelling. Early in the war a city band or members of the local American Legion post might send groups of recruits on their way. Later, as in previous wars, some of the novelty wore off.

Arriving at the fort, recruits were marched to barracks and put to work with mop and broom. The over 200 recruit hutments were Spartan quarters made more unpleasant by impersonal non-commissioned officers who, like many behind the lines warriors, sometimes showed outright contempt for the new soldiers. A more thorough army physical followed the next day, as did the all important Army General Qualification Test. Scores on this test and results of the personal classification interview would determine an eager recruit's future. Most new soldiers, however, gave little effort to the test since it was usually delivered before breakfast. Fort Snelling recruits still scored well above the army average. This meant that a large number of recruits, some 37% in 1943, were assigned to the Air Corps. The practice of skimming the most intelligent recruits for air service was later criticized as it resulted in less intelligent and effective infantrymen.

Following testing, recruits visited one of the clothing warehouses on post for as complete an issue of personal clothing and bedding as was on hand. In 1941 this sometimes meant left over WWI uniforms; supply became more regular shortly thereafter. The excitement of an army uniform faded in the next line as recruits were given their tetanus, smallpox and typhoid injections! An army classification officer next conducted a personal interview, asking about education, prior civilian jobs, hobbies and skills, before submitting recommendations for classification. Until this decision was made, recruits would be drilled, would certainly pull KP and latrine orderly duty and would endure the required chaplain's lecture and orientation films.

When test scores and interview results had been compiled, the recruit's fate was sealed. He might be sent to an individual unit if his skills warranted. Men with high test scores likely were assigned to the Air Corps, at least through 1943. The majority of new recruits were designated for replacement training centers and eventual incorporation into existing units as replacements for casualties. Assigned to ad hoc shipping companies at Fort Snelling, fully processed recruits then

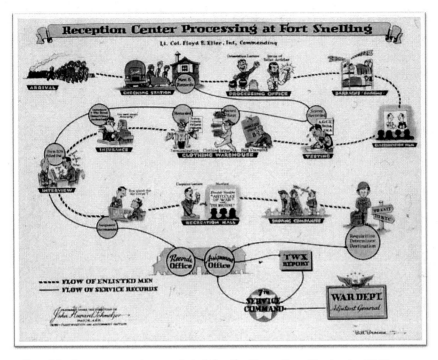

Graphical representations painted for the Reception Center in 1943.

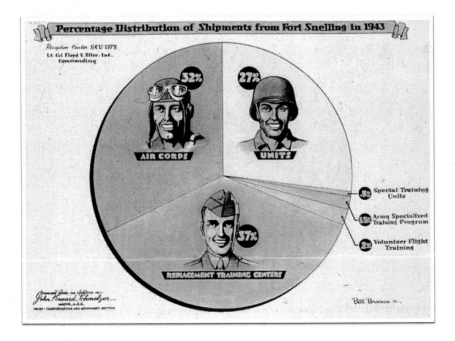

Most inductees left Fort Snelling by train.

awaited their transportation orders. The whole process could take from three days to as long as two weeks.

According to Reception Station commander Lieutenant Colonel Floyd Eller, careful classification and assignment was essential to the war effort: *Every effort must be made to provide each army organization with men that it can use, train and keep. The army must not be forced to undertake useless tasks, such as training clerks to be truck drivers in one place, and truck drivers to be clerks in another; rare experts must not be wasted; organizations must not be given ineffectives who are useless to them; and organization commanders must not be forced to sacrifice training because of initial paper work and administration incident to the reception of new enlisted men.* That was the goal, in any event!

In all nearly 275,000 young men and some women were here inducted into military service during the war years. The Fort Snelling Reception Station grew to its peak in 1942 when a staff of over 1,000 soldiers and civilians were able to fully process as many as 800 recruits each day. Later it would test officer candidates and send combat veterans home on furlough. One of the biggest problems at the fort was simply feeding and housing so many soldiers. Fort Snelling was proud of serving 3,200 meals in 75 minutes and of turning the post field house into an 850 bed dormitory on short notice. And in 1945 and 1946 Fort Snelling's efficiently operating Separation Point was the last taste of army life for tens of thousands of the warriors who helped win World War II.

What might a new recruit see if he were to walk around Fort Snelling during WWII? Over on the Lower Post, the area adjacent to the round tower and the chapel, permanent barracks housed student soldiers of Army units in training. More solidly built old barracks were on the Upper Post, along with the headquarters building with its clock tower and antique cannons on the lawn. Close by were the massive post hospital, fire and police stations, a service club and a movie theatre. Soldiers living in this area felt more fortunate than the recruits in their so called *dog houses* at the Reception Station. Across the wide parade grounds the quartermaster railroad yards received tons of supplies, clothing and food each week.

Linking the Lower and Upper Posts with the Reception Center was the *Fort Snelling Dummy*, an electric streetcar run by well known Francis the Motorman. Off post, soldiers could easily ride city streetcars to the many weekly dances and socials, or they might be lured to the night life in downtown Minneapolis or St. Paul. Back at the fort there were golf, swimming and shooting teams, singing groups and bands, a well equipped gymnasium, and libraries operated by the Red Cross. Many barracks had dayrooms with pool tables, pianos, and writing desks provided by service and church organizations. The air-conditioned post theatre was especially popular with such features as the latest Roy Rogers-Dale Evans movie or Popeye cartoons. The *Fort Snelling Bulletin*, then the oldest post publication in the U.S. Army, each week carried army and local unit news, cartoons, and schedules of activities for the post. Every Sunday KSTP Radio broadcast a *This is the Army* series from the fort, going worldwide on Christmas 1944 with a concert by the fort's choir. *GI Joe*, the popular musical produced by Fort Snelling soldiers, toured the state to raise funds for the Red Cross.

The Fort Snelling "Dummy" electric streetcar, ca. 1930.

Besides welcoming individual soldiers into the army, World War II Fort Snelling was also the birthplace of new specialized military units. Railways were an integral part of the Twin Cities' economy and so it was logical that Fort Snelling should be used to train military railway soldiers. In May 1941, the Headquarters, Military Railway Service was created at the fort with a primary function to *oversee training of military railway troop units and to maintain relations with the commercial railroads under whose supervision the technical training of most of the units was being accomplished.* Each major railway company was to sponsor at least one M.R.S. unit, of which 91 were planned. Newly formed units did their technical training on the job, working side by side with civilian counterparts and learning skills from laying track to dispatching trains to repairing engines. Equally important was the study of foreign railroads systems and careful mapping of foreign lines. The M.R.S. saw important early service in North Africa, where its entire Headquarters was transferred in 1943. Railway battalions trained at Fort Snelling smoothly took over captured railroads and

The Fort Snelling Bulletin *was the nation's oldest post publication.*

running stock and resumed rail supply operations only two days after the North African invasion.

Several military police units also were created at Fort Snelling. Those units designated as Zone of the Interior were responsible for guarding local airports, supply trains and munitions plants, and for transporting prisoners of war and Japanese American so called *enemy aliens* to concentration camps in the Southwest. In September 1942 one of the MP battalions excelled in a surprise exercise, rushing in full combat gear to ordnance plants and strategic points around the Twin Cities. It was only later that they discovered that they had been covering a confidential visit of President Roosevelt to the New Brighton Army Ammunition Plant. The efficiency of Fort Snelling MPs was increased by well trained dogs, including a large poodle, who had themselves attended a training school at the post.

One of the most interesting units which passed through the fort was the 99th Infantry Battalion. Recruits for this organization were expected to have had some experience in snowshoeing and in skiing. But more importantly they were required to be conversant in Norwegian. From Fort Snelling the Battalion traveled to Colorado

A Military Police dog trained at Fort Snelling performs for convalescent soldiers.

for mountain training, yet never spearheaded an invasion of Norway as planned. Rather they fought as line infantrymen across Europe, reaching Norway only after the war and then only to process German soldiers home.

Certainly the most unique and secret part of Fort Snelling's last war was the Military Intelligence Service Language School. Activated at the Presidio of San Francisco in 1941, the school was mandated by early discovery that most military age Japanese Americans had little knowledge of their parents' language. The student body of Nisei, primarily from the West Coast and Hawaii, moved to Camp Savage, Minnesota in May 1941 and occupied the site of the state home for indigent men. Minnesota provided an area with a high degree of racial tolerance

Military Intelligence Service Language School staff and students.

The last retreat, October 1946.

well away from the strongly anti-Japanese West Coast. The program at Camp Savage grew rapidly to include: *reading, writing and speaking Japanese; translation, interpretation and interrogation; captured document analysis; Japanese military and technical terms; Japanese geography and map reading; radio monitoring; social, political, economic, and cultural background of Japan; cursive writing; and order of Battle of the Japanese army.*

By 1944 the school had outgrown Camp Savage and was moved to Fort Snelling with its veil of secrecy finally removed. A decline in recruit processing after the 1943 full mobilization freed up barracks space and from then until the post closed, Fort Snelling assumed a distinctly Japanese-American flavor. The *Post Bulletin* records this change as Nisei names and news stories dominate each weekly issue. Students operated a short-wave radio tuned to Tokyo, and sent regular intelligence reports to Washington, and published an alumni newsletter for graduates in the field. The former post sergeant major reported that the language students were well disciplined and highly motivated soldiers, but that he had to field a few complaints from other soldiers' wives about the strange smells of Japanese cooking in the married quarters.

In 1945 Chinese and Korean language courses were added to the six month and nine month curriculums. Of more interest was the activation of Womens Army Corps sections at Fort Snelling and their full assimilation into the school and post life. After the German surrender, emphasis shifted to spoken Japanese and class work was extended into evenings and weekends, recognizing the critical need for combat translators. After the Japanese surrender the school emphasis again shifted to civil affairs Japanese. Graduates of the school had served with every front-line unit in the Orient, and many of the last of the school's 6,000 graduates working in civil affairs now played an integral part in moving Japan to democracy.

Fort Snelling's last war ended only a year after the shooting stopped. The Separation Point with its enviable record of out processing veterans in 36 hours was closed, and the Intelligence Service Language School moved to Monterey, California. Recruits for the occupation of Europe and Japan would be processed at new locations like Fort McCoy, Wisconsin. Fort Snelling had little continuing utility to an army which needed posts able to handle 30,000 or more men for divisional and combined arms training. On October 15, 1946, the garrison flag in front of post headquarters was lowered for the last time, folded and presented to the wartime post commander Colonel Harry Kealey. Fort Snelling was fading into history.

The years since the war have seen the old World War II and earlier buildings of Fort Snelling used by a variety of agencies: The Veterans' Administration, Bureau of Mines, Department of Natural Resources, General Services Administration, U.S. Army Reserve and the Minnesota Historical Society. Most of the temporary structures are now gone, and all of the old cantonment and recruit processing areas have long been covered by the Twin Cities International Airport. In recent years much of the old artillery area, gun sheds and stables, have been razed for a new sports complex. The prognosis for the rest of the World War II post is mixed but hopeful. Perhaps adaptive uses can preserve this unique campus that has seen so much history and meant so much to generations of Minnesotans.

Fort Snelling's
World War II Buildings

IN SEPTEMBER 1937 MAJOR JOHN HOLT assumed the duties of Fort Snelling quartermaster. He arrived as the Works Progress Administration was busy modernizing buildings, grounds and utilities; by 1939 over $3,000,000 had been expended and nearly every building improved or at least modernized. Holt received support from Seventh Corps to photograph each structure and to produce a new post historical record book, replacing a set begun nearly sixty years earlier. The retired record books and the new set are a unique and detailed account of building improvements spanning a century.

Major Holt also renumbered Fort Snelling's buildings in 1938. Those simplified new numbers used during World War II identify each remaining structure in this guide, with the old letter/number shown in parenthesis. Likewise the building names used by Holt, typically unchanged through the war years, are used but other names from either before or after World War II are shown in brackets.

Third Infantry soldier Jacob Klotzbeacher served at Fort Snelling in the mid 1930s, was again inducted there in 1943, and retired from the Army Reserve there in 1972. Some of his anecdotes of life at the old post are italicized here to help bring life to the Fort Snelling he knew.

The guide is broken into four portions: the Lower Post, the Upper Post areas to the northwest of and to the southeast of the parade grounds, and the areas adjacent to the former Reception Center.

Uncertainty over the future of the Fort Snelling campus precludes suggested tour routes. Roads and access to certain areas are subject to change.

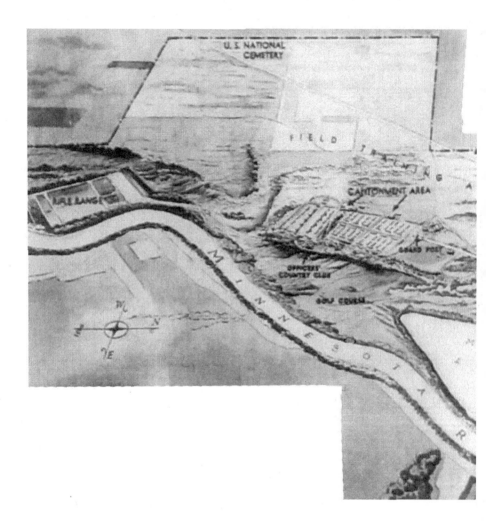

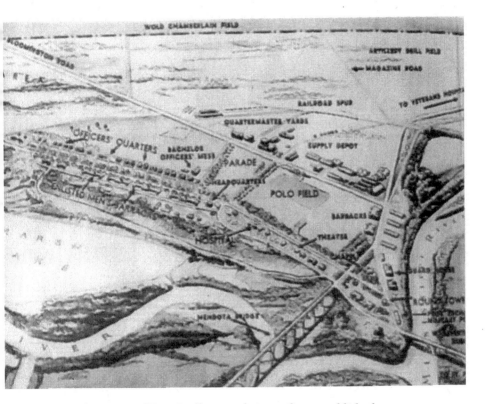

*Perspective view of Fort Snelling on the eve of war, published
in the* Minneapolis Star Journal, *March 9, 1941.*

Amateur historian Sergeant Marian Winter visits the Round Tower, June 1945.

The Lower Post

This area fronting the Mississippi River Valley is the oldest part of Fort Snelling. During the Civil War it was covered with a large number of temporary wooden structures including barracks, warehouses and stables. These were removed as permanent structures were built over the next decades. Many of those wood and brick buildings were in turn removed for highway construction in the 1950s and in development of the Historic Fort Snelling campus in the 1970s.

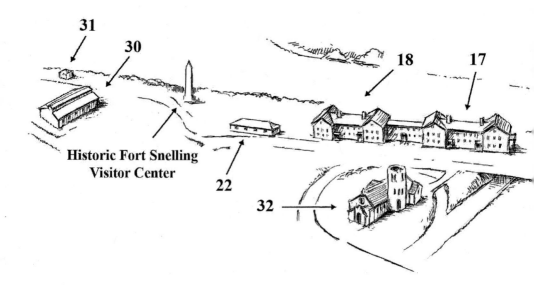

31

30

18

17

**Historic Fort Snelling
Visitor Center**

22

32

Fort Snelling Visitor Center

Built in 1983, this structure houses a large scale model of Fort Snelling in 1945 and is recommended as a starting point for any tour. The underground center sits below what once was a low hill 300 yards from the point of the bluff. Lt. Colonel Henry Leavenworth chose this spot in 1819, the highest ground in the immediate area, as the site for the future Fort Saint Anthony. Colonel Snelling arrived in August 1820 and decided to build at the present site of the restored fort. He laid a cornerstone there the next month.

The Post Cemetery

was established near this spot in 1823 but disused when a new cemetery opened in the 1880s. Graves were moved in 1905 to the new post cemetery, the hill was leveled and wagon storage sheds built on the site. Now the only grave here is that of the famous horse Whiskey whose remains were moved here in 2002 and given a military burial. Whiskey was loved for his many tricks, such as doffing his trainer's cap, picking up a certain colored handkerchief on command, and jumping over a soldier lying on a picnic table. The headstone purchased by officers' wives in 1943 and remains were first moved for Highway 55 construction and moved yet again before the Fort Snelling Light Rail Station was built.

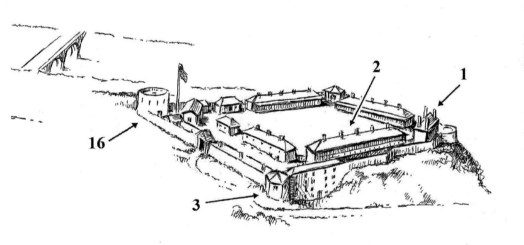

Drawing not to scale

Building 1 (K-1), Commanding Officer's Quarters

The elegant quarters designed and built by Colonel Snelling reflects the style of the New York's Hudson Valley and is probably the oldest extant residence in the state. It was long the symbol of United States influence in the northwest, the scene of countless formal receptions, home to several well known historical figures, and the place where government policy was discussed and administered. Fragments of its 1824 cornerstone were rediscovered by 1970s archaeologists. A columned front porch was added in the 1840s and major improvements made during the Civil War. The roof was raised to a Mansard style in the 1870s. And when the old post was redesigned in 1903 to reflect the Spanish mission style, the commanding officers' quarters received a second story, buff colored stucco and red tile roof, and a full length arched porch. In this configuration it served as field officer quarters and post commander quarters through World War II, and then housed Veterans Administration and Minnesota Historical Society staff until 1975.

All the additions were removed in the late 1970s leaving only a partial shell of original stone with traces of earlier woodwork indicated

W.P.A. retaining walls adjacent to Building 1, ca. 1938.

Comandant's Quarters before restoration to 1825 appearance, ca. 1976.

Commandant's Quarters as restored by the Minnesota Historical Society.

by paint shadows. The house was then carefully restored/reconstructed to its original exterior and conjectural interior appearance. It was soon gutted in a fire that required the entire process to be repeated. Furnished with furniture and accessories appropriate to the 1820s, it today represents the quarters that Abigail and Josiah Snelling called home.

Building 2 (K-2), Field Officers' Quarters

The Officers' Quarters was one of only four original frontier era buildings still standing when Fort Snelling's restoration began in the 1970s. But it was actually the second officers' quarters to stand on the site. In the 1820s a hewn timber structure covered with clapboards housed fourteen sets of quarters and sat on a stone basement level/foundation that contained kitchens. Decrepit and leaking it was replaced by a slightly wider all stone quarters built on the same lower level, the front wall pushed out a few feet. This new 1846 officers' quarters had twelve sets of quarters, each consisting of a parlor, bed chamber and a kitchen in the cellar. A porch, which originally wrapped around each end of the building to the parade ground, now stretched only along the back. Sometime later a full length porch was added to the front.

Like the adjacent Commanding Officers' Quarters, this huge building was converted to a Spanish mission style in 1903 with a second story, full length arched porch, buff stucco and red tile roof.

The redesigned building, now with only six quarters, was continuously occupied until 1975 when this author moved out just prior to restoration. Archaeologists soon removed concrete basement floors to reveal remnants of earlier foundations and fireplaces along with some 28,000 artifacts, providing a glimpse at the material culture and diet of officer families in the 19th century.

Field Officers' Quarters as it looked in 1865 after housing Civil War officers.

The Officers' Quarters looked like a Spanish Mission after 1903.

Officers' Quarters as restored by the Minnesota Historical Society.

Building 3 (K-8), Hexagonal Tower [South Battery]

This limestone defensive tower was designed to protect the front wall and landing road sides of the fort. Mounting cannons on the top floor, the tower could deliver blasts of canister shot the length of each wall. The two lower floors were looped with embrasures, or long slits for muskets, in their outer walls. The South Battery is the least altered of Historic Fort Snelling's four original buildings. During much of the 19th century it was used for storage, though its final military use was as a latrine for a nearby laundress quarters. Later a concrete floor was poured and the tower used to house an electrical transformer.

Hexagonal Tower when it housed a transformer, ca. 1938.

The Tower was the least altered of Fort Snelling's frontier buildings.

Building 16 (K-7), Round Tower

Long the symbol of Fort Snelling, this tower probably constructed in 1820–21 is now the oldest standing building in Minnesota. The Round Tower was designed for last-ditch defense with musket slits that even faced inside the fort's walls. During the Civil War it housed ordnance but was gutted by fire in 1869. The interior was rebuilt, musket slits widened to windows, and crenellations added to the top. Refitted as a guard house it also served for a time served as an office, a prison wash house and for coal storage. In 1903 it was briefly covered in stucco, soon removed. Modified many times both inside and out, the tower finally housed the post electrician whose wife ran a small beauty shop there in the 1930s.

Around 1937 Post Commander Brigadier General C. B. Hodges began converting the tower into a museum with both consent of the War Department and enthusiastic support of post officers and the Works Progress Administration. The new museum, under supervision of the Minnesota Historical Society, opened in the spring of 1941 but was closed for much of World War II. Inside were historical artifacts and displays plus a diagram of the fort built into the terrazzo floor. Around the perimeter of the interior walls were heroic painted panels by artist Richard Haines that depicted the history of the Northwest.

The old round tower museum was gutted in the mid 1960s as the building was excavated and then restored to its presumed 1820s configuration. Today it is part of Historic Fort Snelling and managed by the Minnesota Historical Society.

The Round Tower in 1945.

The Tower with trolley from St. Paul, ca. 1910.

Living room in the Round Tower, 1937.

Round Tower
Museum interior,
ca. 1941.

The flagpole was recently
moved from the Tower
to its 1820s ground level
location.

35

The Post Exchange/Guardhouse, demolished in 1972, once stood just outside the present day reconstructed fort's northwest wall. The West 7th Street Bridge from St. Paul and the trolley line ran in front of the old stone PX originally built in 1864 as a military prison. Many buildings have been in this area over the years: pre-Civil War Dragoon and Artillery stables, Civil War wooden barracks, a bakery, a post trader's store, and warehouses. Later, and through World War II, "officers' row" began near here and extended southwest fronting the Minnesota River Valley. Large red brick duplexes, removed in 1972, were used by field officers and had themselves replaced earlier ornate but hastily constructed 1870s wood frame quarters.

The Post Exchange/Guardhouse, just outside the present fort walls, was removed in 1972.

Building 32 (K-4), Chapel

Soldiers, community groups, area businesses and individuals contributed $50,000 to a chapel fund by 1927, allowing construction of this beautiful structure over the winter of 1927–28. It replaced an older wooden chapel near post headquarters. Built by soldier labor of stone salvaged from piers of the old 1880 Mississippi River Bridge, the new chapel was intended as a community center for the entire post. During the 1930s this numbered about 2,000 troops in winter and 7,000 in summer. The Fort Snelling Chapel was the first U.S. Army church erected by community subscription and the first pan-sectarian chapel at an Army garrison. Memorial stained glass windows commemorate the history of the area and flags of historical military units with local connections hang from the rafters. The front entrance with interior steps was added later to the original construction.

Intended to serve the civilian community and located at the center of the Twin Cities park system, it still fulfills its religious function every Sunday morning and is frequently used for weddings and funerals. While on state property and now managed by the Minnesota Department of Natural Resources, it is actively supported by the Fort Snelling Memorial Chapel Foundation.

Military wedding at original Chapel entrance, ca. 1930.

Chapel, ca. 1934.

A new covered entrance was constructed in the early 1930s.

Buildings 17 (K-11) and 18 (K-12), Barracks

In 1904 Congress authorized over $10 million in construction funds for military posts and in 1905, as part of the largest peacetime budget in the army's history, over $11 million for construction. Fort Snelling soon embarked on a huge construction boom with new barracks for cavalry and artillery, stables and quartermaster buildings. Many of these solidly built structures still stand while others, like two nearby artillery barracks, were removed for highway or airport construction.

Fort Snelling was designated a regimental post in 1902 with separate campuses for an infantry regiment and smaller artillery and cavalry units. The latter was on the lower post and included two barracks, officers' quarters, horse stables and guard houses.

These 44 x 150 foot buildings with two 39 x 59 foot wings were built as double barracks divided by firewalls in 1904-05 on the site of earlier wooden barracks. They were built to a standard War Department plan featuring a central structure flanked by wings and with two tiered verandas. Each side housed 85 men or one cavalry troop, and a solid fire wall divided each half building. While cavalry permanently left the post in 1911, the barracks continued to be occupied by permanent party troops. Soldier labor completed an addition and modifications to each building in 1935–36, filling the courtyard between the wings and increasing the capacity to two now larger companies or 218 men. These barracks were home to machine gun companies of 3rd Infantry in 1930s, to companies in training early in World War II, and to Intelligence Service Language School students in 1944–46. For many years following the war the buildings were used as outpatient clinics for the Veterans' Administration, which added the link between the barracks.

Cavalrymen inside Building 17, ca. 1910.

Each building's two wings were connected with new construction in 1936.

Building 18 with trolley tracks to Minneapolis, spring 1946.

The Fatigue uniform was a real monstrosity. It was ill-fitting, made of blue denim consisting of a shapeless hat (looking like a soup bowl with fringes), a denim jacket and blue jeans. The jacket fit like a tent with sleeves, and the jeans fit like something worn by an underground balloon corps. (J.K.)

41

The two barracks were linked with a three level passageway ca. 1947.

Building 22 (F-1), Ordnance Warehouse [Ordnance Storehouse]

Built in 1878-80 as an ordnance warehouse, this 26 X 100 stone structure has a partial basement. At about the time the warehouse was built
the crumbling exterior walls of the frontier fort were being systemati-
cally removed. Recycled limestone blocks quarried by soldier labor
in the 1820s were used for new construction like this warehouse and
for foundations for other new buildings, thus speeding the work and
saving money. The warehouse was later used by the quartermaster
to issue clothing. During World War II it housed a photo shop, shoe
shop, tailor house and warehouse for the nearby Post Exchange. The
Veterans' Administration used the old building as an orthopedic brace
construction shop for many years after the war, and today it is used as
a warehouse and maintenance workshop.

*After about three days, three of us fellows from the group were
assigned to "H" Company, 3rd Infantry of the Old Guard, as machine
gunners. The 3rd Infantry Regiment is the oldest organized military unit in the U.S. Army, which was organized 1784 from units of
George Washington's Continental Army. They took us down to the
quartermaster supply depot and issued us some ill-fitting uniforms.
I got several pair of shorts of at least size 44. (My waist at that time
was size 32). These shorts reached below my knees. After three months
in the service, having completed basic training, I was entitled to a
Class "A" uniform. We went down to get measured up for the Class
"A" so the guys got a look at my shorts and just about died laughing.
They said, "Who in the hell issued you your uniform?" I told them,
"Some of your screwy buddies!" (J.K.)*

Ordnance Warehouse, ca. 1938.

Lean-to additions date to the early 20th century.

Building 30 (F-37), Service Company Garage
[Horse Stable, Post Garage]

The last of four nearly identical cavalry stables originally on the site, this 67 x 160 foot brick structure originally held 82 horse stalls for one troop of cavalry. A hay loft extended the length of the upper level. In 1936 the building was converted to the Post Garage with large doors on the northwest side. It now held 33 vehicles and a repair shop. Following closure of the post in 1946 Building 30 was retrofitted by the Veterans Administration to serve as outpatient clinics. The Minnesota Historical Society in turn has used the structure for storage since the State of Minnesota acquired most of the Lower Post in the late 1960s. [The other three stables were removed in 1983 for construction of the Fort Snelling History Center parking lot. Also on this site during World War II were 2 brick stable guardhouses, wooden wagon sheds and 2 large red brick artillery barracks, now all gone.]

Exercising cavalry horses, ca. 1906.

Post Garage, ca. 1938.

Building 31 (K-10), Ordnance Warehouse
[Ordnance Magazine, Dog House]

The little 10 x 12 foot stone structure was built in 1905 to hold ammunition for the cavalry. It reportedly finished out its military years as a dog house for one of the post commanders. The roof and door were burned by vandals but the surviving walls stabilized by the Minnesota Historical Society.

Former Ordnance Warehouse, ca. 1938.

An everyday sight at the Fort Snelling warehouses.

Quartermaster Yards/ Supply Depot

Before Minnesota Highway 55 bisected the post the entire area northwest of the old frontier fort was known as the Upper Post because its higher elevation ground was further up the Minnesota River valley. The grand vision for the Upper Post was proposed by General Alfred H. Terry, commanding the Department of Dakota headquartered at the fort in 1883. Secretary of War Robert Todd Lincoln obtained an appropriation of $112,500 which expanded new construction that had started there in 1879.

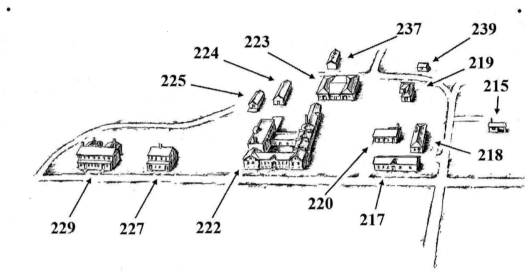

The Upper Post consisted of an artillery campus with barracks, stables, gun sheds and workshops and a quartermaster campus further
northwest that included more stables, wagon sheds, and a variety of
workshops and warehouses. On the other side of the huge artillery and
infantry parade grounds, later reconstituted as sports fields and a golf
course, were headquarters, administrative and infantry housing areas
described in a following section.

At its peak size in 1945, Fort Snelling spread up the Minnesota Valley past the present International Airport. A huge Reception Station there encompassed over 200 buildings. Other permanent buildings spread west from the present fence at the end of Taylor Avenue. All of these buildings were removed when the International Airport was established in 1969.

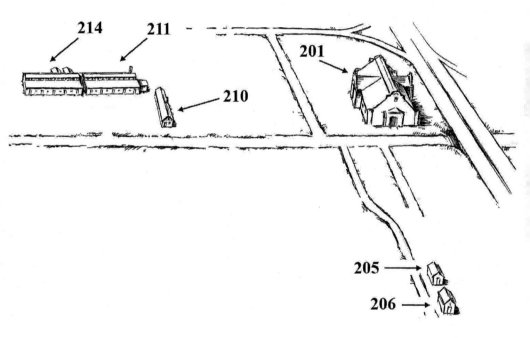

Building 201 (F-42), Riding Hall
[Cavalry Drill Hall/Field House]

Minnesota winters can be unforgiving and heavy snow restrictive to cavalry and horse drawn artillery drills. Built in 1907 as an indoor drill hall for one troop of cavalry, the new building was damaged by a tornado in 1914 but later improved with a spectators' platform in 1922 and a heating system in 1926. Both cavalry and artillery troops drilled here in the winter, and veterans reported horse drawn cannons and caissons moving so fast that they ran on only one wheel in the turns.

The hall was also an excellent venue for live shows that provided entertainment in the days before radio and television. By WWII the massive 108 x 244 foot structure was now called the Field House and was used for large post gatherings to which civilians were frequently invited. A concrete floor treated for dancing had been laid in 1941, a 32 x 40 foot stage built, and a thousand folding chairs purchased to augment theater seating installed earlier. Soon live entertainment programs were being broadcast over the radio. In October 1945 it was briefly used as a barrack for 850 men who were here to be processed into service.

Following years of use as a large scale testing laboratory for the United States Bureau of Mines, and a failed conversion to a sports complex, the building and grounds were sold to the Northern Star Council of the Boy Scouts of America. Extensive restoration, conversion and grounds work has ensured its useful life for many more years as an urban retreat for young people to learn outdoor and leadership skills.

The exterior bricks are covered with names, dates and inscriptions left by Fort Snelling soldiers over the years.

One of many historically inscribed bricks.

The Riding Hall, ca. 1938.

Polo game, ca. 1937.

Flag Day, 1942.

Polo players, ca. 1937.

The big Post Fieldhouse, 1946.

Parade Grounds/Sports Fields

Originally gardens, these large fields were later Civil War era camping and training grounds. As the post expanded a parade ground for horse drawn artillery and another for infantry maneuvers were developed on either side of Minnehaha Avenue. By the late 1920s use of the grounds had expanded to recreational fields with baseball diamonds, a running track, and polo fields. It was here that horse shows, field days and polo games attracted thousands of civilian spectators. The W.P.A. raised and leveled the old drill fields in the late 1930s, and the field was lighted and a concrete stadium finished just before World War II.

Sports on the post were very limited during the Depression years. The Army had few funds to spend on athletic activities. They did start a boxing program in the Fall of '35, which I took part in. We trained all winter, but nothing ever came of it. No matches were ever scheduled. Training took place in a building called the Riding Hall which is still in existence today. They used to train horses in it. (J.K.)

Artillery officer trainees practice artillery drill, 1918.

Building 205 (F-27) and 206 (F-28), Workshops
[Artillery Work Shops]

Between long wooden artillery storage sheds, no longer extant, were
2 smaller red brick artillery workshops, constructed in 1903 of brick
over stone foundations. Each of the two 20 x 45 foot structures was
designed for three artisans who shoed artillery horses among other
duties. The workshops were moved east to the far edge of the ball fields
to serve the newly configured sports fields.

Artillery Workshop, ca. 1938.

**Buildings 202 and 207, Artillery and Tank Storage Sheds/
Stables,** along Bloomington Road, were built in 1903 as artillery
storage sheds each designed to hold 17 horse drawn field pieces.
Behind were stables, some of which were destroyed by a 1939 fire that
killed most of the superbly trained horses and prompted mechanization and reassignment of the artillery to another post. Two temporary buildings just across from the Field House (T203 and T203A)
were put up in 1940 as motor transport sheds. This area was the Post
Motor Pool after mechanization of the army. All these buildings were
removed in 2000 to make way for parking lots and new construction.

Aftermath of tragic 1939 stables fire.

Building 210 (F-43), Ordnance and Civil Works Services Office and Warehouse [Quartermaster Shops]

This brick building on a stone foundation, measuring 28 x 150 feet with a partial basement, was built 1907 to house five workshops for the Quartermaster Department. With the 1936 removal of several electric motors used to power workshop tools it was converted into a warehouse and office.

We didn't keep much of an army after World War I. There weren't supposed to be any more wars. In the 1930s, we hadn't improved the armed forces. We were wearing WWI uniforms and had mostly horse and mule-drawn vehicles. Weapons were basically the same. A few units were being mechanized. At least they were getting trucks to do the hauling and to pull artillery pieces. (J.K.)

The Quartermaster Shops as constructed, ca. 1910.

Office and Warehouse, ca. 1938.

Building 211 (F-49), Tank Park
[Quartermaster Stables, Tank and Motor Sheds]

Built as a quartermaster stable with capacity of 106 animals in 1909, the structure held six box stalls and 100 individual stalls for the work animals used to draw supply wagons. It was damaged in the 1914 tornado and then a devastating June 1916 fire mostly destroyed the 67 x 195 foot building with its hay loft above. Rebuilt as a stable, it was later converted to use as a garage for 42 vehicles including the little World War I era tanks of Fort Snelling's 7th Tank Company.

The 7th Tank Company finally received modern machines in 1937.

Tank Park, ca. 1938.

Building 214 (F-56), Veterinary Hospital and Quartermaster Warehouse [Quartermaster Stables/Motor Repair Shop]

Another quartermaster stable, this 67 x 95 foot brick building was completed in 1910. Its six box stalls and 100 individual stalls had a capacity of 106 animals. Hay was stored in a loft above. In 1923 the building was altered with conversion of a portion into a veterinary wing, complete with operating suite. Now its capacity was 13 animals in the hospital and 74 in the main stable. Partially burned in 1931, it resumed its hospital role with a lab for the Post Veterinarian installed in 1938 and two small wings constructed at an unknown date. Before World War II it became yet another motor repair shop and warehouse as the army converted to motorized transportation. It was later used as a medical research facility by the Veterans Administration.

Veterinary Hospital, ca. 1930.

Building 215 (F-57), Quartermaster Gas Station

The gas pumps that filled government trucks were operated from this 12 x 24 foot cement structure completed in 1932. New pumps were installed in 1938 to draw from underground storage tanks with capacity of 32,445 gallons.

Quartermaster Gas Station, ca. 1938.

Building 217 (F-7), Quartermaster Warehouse [Quartermaster Storehouse/Plumbing Shop]

Ambiguous records indicate a date as early as 1879 but the structure more likely dates to World War I or even later. The 19th century wooden warehouse on this site, a 25 x 100 foot structure, featured a large wagon scale at the north end of building and a loading dock that ran entire length of the side facing Bloomington Road. In 1938 the building was listed as a quartermaster salvage warehouse.

Our uniforms consisted of three classes. The Class-A, which was our issued dress uniform, was well-tailored of fine, woven wool. It also consisted of a garrison cap (visor type), a blouse with a brown belt, a cotton shirt with shoulder tabs, britches, and rolled leggings, with well-fitting garrison type shoes (color, light brown). We were also issued slacks to be worn for dress with this uniform, but had to wear britches and leggings at all official functions.

The Class-B uniform consisted of a campaign hat, rough wool shirt, britches, leggings and a combat-type rugged shoe. This uniform was worn for drill and generally around the area, but not off post.

We were also issued a flimsy raincoat, an overcoat made of the same rough wool as the Class-B uniform, and a couple black neckties, several pairs of under-shirts, shorts and socks. There was also field equipment, such as a webbed belt, pack, canteen, blankets, holster and a 45-caliber semiautomatic pistol. (J.K.)

Quartermaster Warehouse, ca. 1938.

Building 218 (F-11), Civilian Conservation Corps Warehouse [Quartermaster Warehouse/Forage House]

In 1933 the Army helped mobilize and operate over 1,300 Civilian Conservation Corps camps nationwide. While regular army officers initially commanded C.C.C. units, Reserve officers were directing operations within two years. While Europe moved toward war, the C.C.C. experience prepared over 300,000 American men for eventual military service. The Supply Company of the Minnesota District C.C.C., later designated the Headquarters Company, had its offices in Fort Snelling's quartermaster complex and managed up to 300 men. Their workers and hundreds of additional men from the Works Progress Administration labored over four years to replace the post's crumbling utilities, reroof most of the buildings, build miles of drainage ditches, add wooden garages behind most of the quarters, and replace decayed wooden porches, steps and railings with functional concrete.

This 22 x 77 foot brick quartermaster warehouse was built in 1894 to hold 40 tons of hay and 50 tons of oats for Quartermaster Department work animals. It continued in use as a quartermaster warehouse for other supplies as the army mechanized and was transferred to control of the Civilian Conservation Corps in 1933.

C.C.C. Warehouse, ca. 1938.

Building 220 (F-58), Post Exchange Gas Station [Oil and Gas Station/Auto Repair Shop]

A tiny wooden quartermaster gas station built in 1928 was replaced only four years later by this rusticated cement block, 11.5 x 60 foot, more modern facility constructed with Post Exchange funds. It continued operation under civilian management for decades after the post was closed.

Quartermaster Gas Station, ca. 1938.

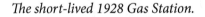

The short-lived 1928 Gas Station.   *Gas Station addition, ca. 1937.*

Building 219 (F-10), Wheelwright Shop [Sawmill]

As the Indian Wars wound down by 1895 only 80 posts remained garrisoned even though annual army funding remained at over one million dollars. Thus Fort Snelling continued to grow thanks to consolidation elsewhere. New Quartermasters Department Buildings 218, 219 and 239 were constructed in this era.

Built of limestone in 1895 this 19.5 x 40 foot tin roofed building housed skilled artisans who operated saws to custom fabricate timbers. In the next few years wheelwrights were added who repaired cannon and wagon wheels. It was partially destroyed by fire on Christmas day 1913, and then damaged by a tornado the following year. It was rebuilt with a forge for use of a blacksmith. Electric motors were moved here from Building 210 in 1936 and the building may have continued use as a shop during World War II. In more recent years to was used for smoke filled building training by the Veterans Administration Fire Department.

Wagons awaiting repair, ca. 1905.

Wheelwright Shop, ca. 1938.

Building 239 (F-15), Oil House [Mineral Oil House]

One of the few stone structures on post, this 19 x 33 foot building featured a corrugated sheet iron roof and a dirt floor. Built in 1892, it was designed to hold 10,000 gallons of oil used in lighting the post's many oil lamps. It was repaired after damage by the 1914 tornado.

Oil House, ca. 1905.

Building 223 (F-61), Civilian Conservation Corps Warehouse [Quartermaster Storehouse, Fort Snelling Fire Station]

This concrete block structure, 130 x 135 feet, was built in 1935 specifically for the C.C.C. It replaced a wooden quartermaster storehouse from World War I and was last used by the Veterans' Administration Fire Department.

C.C.C. Warehouse, ca. 1938.

Building 237 (F-2), Granary
[Powder Magazine/Grain Shed]

Corrugated sheet iron on stone piers was used to build this unusual structure in 1904. It may have been initially located elsewhere, and moved to this location in 1931. Fenced off and guarded, it was

Powder Magazine, ca. 1905.

designed to hold 450 pounds of gunpowder but apparently was soon redesignated to hold grain for Quartermaster Department animals. During World War II it likely served as a warehouse.

Granary, ca. 1938.

Building 224 (F-16), Utilities Shops
[Forage House/Utility Shops and Warehouse]

Built in 1902 to hold 285 tons of baled hay and 350 tons of oats for Quartermaster Department animals, the 35 x 185 foot brick building divided by a firewall was converted only four years later into workshops. The C.C.C. added a basement, new doors and windows, and four loading platforms in 1936.

Some of our daily tasks were: K.P., stable detail (where we fed, groomed and cleaned up), area police, firemen (who kept all the buildings warm by shoveling coal, hauling ashes, etc.), snow shoveling in winter (without snow blowers), manicuring the parade grounds and all officers' yards in summertime with push mowers, changing and cleaning of windows on all post buildings in the Spring, as well as maintenance painting by paint crews. (J.K.)

C.C.C. workers, late 1930s.

*Utilities Shops and
Warehouse, ca. 1938.*

*Utilities Shops and
Warehouse.*

Building 225 (F-60), Paint Shop
[Quartermaster Storehouse]

In 1917 during World War I a temporary 20.5 x 77 foot wooden warehouse was built here on cement and wooden piers. In 1928 it was redesignated

Warehouse as built, ca. 1917.

as a permanent building and given a new block foundation. Through World War II and beyond it served as a paint shop for the post. A dedicated storage building was essential because of the highly flammable nature of paints used at that time.

Paint Shop, ca. 1938.

Building 222 (F-14, 18, 19) Bakery, Commissary, Quarter-master Office and Warehouse
[Root House/ Subsistence Storehouse/ Quartermaster Warehouse]

This large complex is composed of several connected buildings, each with multiple uses and modifications over the years. It began as twin brick warehouses, one for quartermaster and the other for commissary use, built perpendicular to Bloomington Road. Most of the original 32 x 180 foot brick quartermaster building built in 1904 burned down in November 1929. A replacement building (F-19), 144 x 145 feet, went up in 1935 as a multi story, flat roofed warehouse utilizing

Quartermaster Warehouse, 1915.

the small front portion of the original structure that survived the fire.

The brick subsistence storehouse and quartermaster office parallel to it on the northeast (F-18), 32 x 178 feet, was constructed in 1905. In 1938 it was used as a commissary sales store and warehouse.

A 1914 annex parallel to Bloomington Road connected the two large warehouses. Train tracks from a spur line begun in 1903 allowed easy unloading of supplies into the several long warehouses on either side.

A one story 35 x 100 foot brick root house (F-14) was constructed against the west end of F-18 in 1905 to hold an annual supply of vegetables. In 1937 Works Progress Administration laborers converted this structure into a new post bakery to replace the old bakery (Building 112) recently converted to married non commissioned officer quarters.

The General Services Administration continued to use the complex as warehouses for decades after World War II.

Above right: After the 1929 fire, a new warehouse was built in 1935.

Right: The 1905 Root House converted to a bakery in 1937.

Building 227 (F-30, 31), Non-commissioned Officers' Quarters

Two senior non-commissioned officers, who presumably worked in the warehouses, occupied this 1904 Colonial Revival style duplex with their families. The so called double set of quarters measured around 27 x 37.5 feet and featured a full length open front porch with white wooden pillars. Like most buildings on post, part of its wooden trim was replaced in brick and concrete and the porch was enclosed by W.P.A. laborers in 1938.

The NCO duplex as built, ca. 1905.

Non-commissioned Officers' Quarters, ca. 1938.

Building 229 (F-38, 39, 40, 41), Non-commissioned Officers' Quarters

Four non-commissioned officers, who presumably worked in the warehouses, lived in this Colonial Revival style so called four set of quarters with their families. The 27 x 76 foot building likewise had its porch enclosed and wooden trim replaced by the W.P.A. in 1938.

One of the door nameplates reads Wilbur G. Grippen who lived there as a Veterans Administration employee until the 1970s. But his experiences at Fort Snelling began in the 1930s as a high school student attending one of the Citizens Military Training Camps, then later as a World War inductee at the post. Following his discharge he stayed at Fort Snelling working for the Veterans Administration that occupied many of the old post buildings, including these quarters.

The NCO four set of quarters as built, ca. 1905.

Non-commissioned Officers' Quarters, ca. 1938.

Convalescent soldiers at Fort Snelling Hospital, ca. 1945

The Upper Post

Before Minnesota Highway 55 bisected the post, the entire area northwest of the old frontier fort was known as the Upper Post because its higher elevation ground was further up the Minnesota River valley. This area fronting the valley consisted of post headquarters and a variety of administrative and support buildings, infantry barracks, and officers' quarters.

On the other side of the huge artillery and infantry parade grounds were an artillery campus with barracks, stables, gun sheds and workshops and a quartermaster campus further northwest that included more stables, wagon sheds, and a variety of workshops and warehouses.

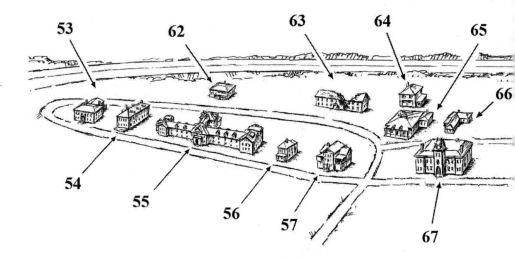

Parade Grounds/Sports Fields

These large fields served as Civil War era camping and training grounds. As the post expanded a parade ground for horse drawn artillery and another for infantry maneuvers were developed on either side of Minnehaha Avenue. By the late 1920s use of the grounds had expanded to recreational fields with baseball diamonds, a running track, and polo fields. It was here that horse shows, field days and polo games attracted thousands of civilian spectators.

A golf course was built over the infantry parade grounds and originally extended all the way west to the Officers' Country Club. The W.P.A. raised and leveled the old drill fields in the late 1930s, and the field was lighted and a concrete stadium finished just before World War II.

Near the junction of Taylor Avenue and Minnehaha Avenue was a tower that broadcast recorded bugle calls to announce changes in the military duty. The live bugler had been replaced just before the war. And at the nearby flagpole, the stars and stripes were officially lowered for the last time on October 15, 1946.

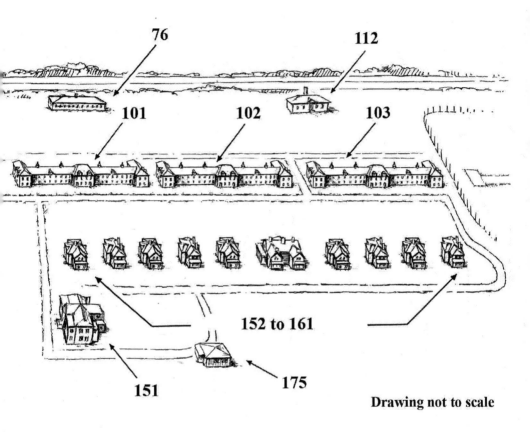

76   112

101   102   103

152 to 161

151   175

Drawing not to scale

Building 151 (A-20), Officers' Quarters, 9 sets [Bachelor Officers' Quarters]

Unmarried Fort Snelling junior officers typically shared quarters in the same types of buildings that housed married officers. Rank and seniority determined who got the largest/newest/best quarters and "bumping" was an old tradition. In 1904 the first dedicated bachelor officers' quarters were constructed as a 33 x 140 foot brick structure with a 33 x 45 foot wing and designed to house ten officers. An officers' club was opened on the first floor the next year. A 12 x 12.5 foot kitchen addition for married officers was built in 1929, and more additions or wings added later to eventually bring the building's capacity to 38 bachelor and four married officers by the outbreak of World War II.

Bachelor Officers' Quarters, ca. 1910.

Bachelor Officers' Quarters, ca. 1938.

Bachelor Officers' Quarters, ca. 1938.

Well, Army life wasn't so bad, but it seemed like someone else was in charge of your life. You were made to believe the officers were some sort of gods. They thought so too. This has changed a lot. In the old days, few of us had more than an eighth-grade education. (J.K.)

Building 175, Clubhouse

In late 1940 or early 1941 this temporary style wooden structure was erected to serve golfers using the adjacent nine hole course, which had recently been modified by the W.P.A. Next to the flagpole is a stone marker to the Treaty of 1837 signed at Fort Snelling in which the Dakota, Ojibwa and Winnebago tribes ceded land from the Mississippi River east to the St. Croix. As settlers flooded in pressure grew on the United States to reduce the size of the huge Fort Snelling military reservation.

Golf Course Clubhouse, 2009.

Officers of any rank had some private or PFC to keep his boots and leather shined, plus doing other menial chores for him. Sometimes they would give the guy a few cents, but it wasn't required. These orderlies were known as "dog robbers." In those days, all the buildings were heated with coal. The soldiers were expected to keep the fires going during the winter. Now days, civilians are hired to help keep the army post functioning. (J.K.)

Building 152 (A-1), Officer's Quarters

The army enforced a social and physical separation between officers and enlisted personnel during the 19th century and through World War II. This side of Taylor Avenue, named for later president Colonel Zachary Taylor who commanded Fort Snelling in 1828, featured picket fences, ornamental plantings, and a wide setback from the road. Sweeping lawns, curved drives and sidewalks and the street offset differentiated *officers' territory* from the enlisted men across the street.

Individual quarters and duplexes were constructed along Taylor Avenue in 1879, 1892, and 1905. Much of the highly decorative trim features on the quarters were removed during W.P.A. renovation in the late 1930s. After the post closed in 1946 the houses were used by Veterans Administration doctors and staff until the early 1970s. The quarters originally extended much further to the west with twelve additional structures demolished when the airport expanded in 1969.

Major General Bundy outside his quarters, ca. 1895.

Built in the original 1879–80 construction phase, this 32 x 52 foot brick quarters housed one officer and family and is of a different design than the quarters later constructed.

Officer's Quarters, ca. 1938.

Building 153 (A-2), Officer's Quarters

Built in 1892, the 36 X 60 foot brick quarters housed one officer and family. It was first of a series of 1892 quarters built in the spaces between the earlier 1879-80 quarters.

Officer's Quarters as they looked, ca. 1905.

Officer's Quarters, ca. 1938.

Building 154 (A-3), Officer's Quarters

Built in 1879–80, the 32 x 56 foot brick quarters housed one officer and family.

Officer's Quarters as they looked, ca. 1905.

Officer's Quarters, ca. 1938.

Building 155 (A-4), Officer's Quarters

Built in 1892, the 32 x 52 foot brick quarters housed one officer and family.

Officer's Quarters as they looked, ca. 1905.

Officer's Quarters, ca. 1938.

Building 156 (A-5), Officer's Quarters [Nurses' Quarters]

Built in 1879–80, the 38 x 56 foot brick quarters originally housed one officer and family. In 1938 it was converted to house eleven nurses who worked in the station hospital complex.

Officer's Quarters as they looked, ca. 1905.

Officer's Quarters, ca. 1938.

Building 157 (A-21, 22), Officers' Quarters, Double Set [Officers' Quarters, Double Set]

Built in 1905, the 24 x 66 foot brick double quarters with 19.5 x 21 foot wings housed two officers and their families.

Officers' Quarters, Double Set, as they looked ca. 1905.

Officers' Quarters, Double Set, ca. 1938.

Building 158 (A-6), Officer's Quarters

Built in 1879–80, the 32 x 56 foot brick quarters housed one officer and family.

Officer's Quarters as they looked, ca. 1905.

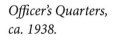

Officer's Quarters, ca. 1938.

Building 159 (A-7), Officer's Quarters

Built in 1892, the 36 x 60 foot brick quarters housed one officer and family.

Officer's Quarters, as they looked, ca. 1905.

Officer's Quarters, ca. 1938.

Building 160 (A-8), Officer's Quarters

Built in 1879–80, the 32 x 56 foot brick quarters housed one officer and family.

Officer's Quarters as they looked, ca. 1905.

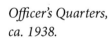

Officer's Quarters, ca. 1938.

Building 161 (A-9), Officer's Quarters

Built in 1892, the 36 x 60 foot brick quarters housed one officer and family.

Officer's Quarters as they looked, ca. 1905.

Officer's Quarters, ca. 1938.

Building 112 (L-11), Quartermaster Warehouse [Post Bakery]

Centered behind the row of infantry barracks that once fronted Taylor Avenue was the important post bakery. Built in 1891, it measured 31 x 61 feet and turned out thousands of loaves of bread each week for hungry soldiers.

Post Bakery, ca. 1905.

A 31 x 21 foot wing was added to the brick structure later, and it was finally converted into non-commissioned officers' quarters in 1937. Nearby were a swimming pool and tennis courts for use of the enlisted men quartered in the long row of barracks. The "Dummy Line" streetcar ran the entire length of the post from the main Post Exchange on the lower post out to the cantonment. Its tracks were between the barracks and in front of the old post bakery.

Quartermaster Warehouse, ca. 1938.

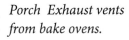

Porch Exhaust vents from bake ovens.

103

Building103 (B-3), Barracks, 2 Companies
[Infantry Barracks/ Barracks, Double Set]

In 1944 this barrack was Headquarters of the 744th Railway Operating Battalion and later used as classrooms. Like the other barracks, it housed Army Reserve units until 1981. Jacob Klotzbeacher, whose italicized reminiscences of 1935 life at Fort Snelling illustrate these pages, retired from this building in 1972 as a U.S. Army Reserve first sergeant.

The next barrack, 105 and no longer standing, was identical to the previous three. Two additional square shaped permanent brick barracks lay beyond. One of these housed the enlisted faculty and cadre of the Military Intelligence Service Language School during the second half of WWII. These three barracks and the corresponding officers' quarters across from them were removed by construction of the Twin Cities International Airport in the 1960s.

Typical barracks interior at Fort Snelling, ca. 1941.

Officer candidates in morning formation, 1917.

Anyway, the first morning at Fort Snelling we got our initial introduction into Army life. They took us out to police up the area, (pick up cigarette butts, etc.). At breakfast we were all given a pint of milk. This came in small bottles with sort of a pressed paper cork in it. I'd never encountered milk in a bottle before, so I looked quizzically at this cork, thinking "How in the blazes do I open this?" I then recalled someone telling me that if you pushed a knife handle down one side, the seal would turn on edge, and you'd be able to pull it out. So I picked up my knife, took aim and gave it all I had, which was more than plenty. Half the milk came out with the cork and went all over the table, soaking the guys around me who were dressed in Class "A" uniforms. I was embarrassed to death. There heard remarks like "damned hillbilly" along with murmurs about dry cleaning uniforms. I had myself pictured going to the guard house! (J.K.)

MISLS student Bud Nakasone outside Building 102, 1946.

Building 102 (B-2), Barracks, 2 Companies
[Infantry Barracks/ Barracks, Double Set]

Nearly identical to barracks on either side, this barrack like the others served as a row ward when Fort Snelling became U.S. Reconstruction General Hospital 29 in the wake of the First World War. It alternately housed military trainees during World War II and served as classrooms for students of the Military Intelligence Service Language School. During the 1960s and until 1981 the barracks and many other old Fort Snelling structures were the home to a number of U.S. Army Reserve units.

Officer candidates practice bayonet fencing, 1917.

Building 101 (B-1), Barracks, 2 Companies
[Infantry Barracks/ Barracks, Double Set]

With late 19th century reductions in military posts, only 119 garrisons remained by 1884. Some of the largest posts were close to larger cities. Nearly a quarter million dollars was appropriated in 1885 to build nearly 100 new military buildings nationwide, and the four identical double barracks likely came from these funds. The fourth, Building 105, is no longer extant.

The massive barracks, 49 x 301 feet with 22 x 88 foot wings, were constructed between 1885 and 1889. Built as double sets for two companies, 65 men on each side, they had solid fire walls between. Detached kitchens were in the rear. A W.P.A. addition in 1935 raised the capacity of the barracks to 236 men.

I must say that we ate quite well in the Army in those days compared to the general civilian population. This was during the heart of the Depression; there were soup kitchens set up in the cities to feed the homeless. Many still had homes, but no food. (J.K.)

These were the first barracks on post to have steam heat and indoor restrooms, and became home to the Third United States Infantry known as The Old Guard which arrived on post in 1888.

In the Fall, we put on parades every Tuesday and Friday. Tuesdays there were battalion parades and Fridays were regimental parades. These were normally in the evening so people from Minneapolis and St. Paul could enjoy them after work. We had mules and horses in the parades also. For example, in the machine gun unit, there were mules hooked to the machine gun carts, munitions carts, water carts, and so on. After the parade we had all that stuff to clean up and put away, wash all the carts, groom the mules, and wash the harnesses with saddle soap. All in all, they managed to keep us busy (J.K.)

*Infantry Barracks,
ca. 1938.*

*Soldiers enjoy a
game of crack the
whip, 1935.*

Building 76 (F-4), Non Commissioned Officers' Quarters [Civilian Employees' Quarters]

While the records indicate that this 31 x 148 foot brick structure was erected in 1879 to house four employees and their families, it is not known if this is in any part the original building. The quarters were extensively rebuilt in 1938 to serve as non-commissioned officers' quarters.

Wooden additions are no longer present.

Non-commissioned Officers' Quarters, ca. 1938.

Building 66 (C-13), Signal Corps Office and Barracks [Telephone Exchange and Signal Building]

The original 22 x 57 foot brick building was put up in 1927. Phones were a relatively new item at the turn of the century and were just becoming widespread in the 1920s. The building was given a 27 x 80.5 foot addition in 1939 and now contained barracks for 16 men, a film library and a photo lab. Its personnel showed training films to a reported 660,000 troops during World War II.

Building 66, Army switchboard operators, 1941.

Signal Corps Office as constructed, ca. 1927.

Signal Corps Office and Barracks, ca. 1938.

Building 67 (C-1), Post Headquarters [Headquarters, Department of Dakota/Administration Building]

Since 1866 military Department of Dakota headquarters had been in downtown St. Paul. But in 1878 a general order required all such headquarters be moved to the nearest military post. Fort Snelling was then in poor condition, with few improvements since the Civil War. Two years later Minnesotan Alexander Ramsey, then Secretary of War, and Commanding General William T. Sherman began reductions in the number of forts and concentrated investments on fewer strategic posts. Meanwhile $100,000 had been appropriated to build a head-quarters, a new commanding officer quarters, and twelve more quarters to house staff officers. Another $100,000 was soon appropriated to further develop the new Upper Post.

The beautiful headquarters building was built in 1880–81 at a cost of $27,000. It served as Department of Dakota headquarters, then responsible for the command and supply of many smaller posts as far west as Montana. Troops could be dispatched from Fort Snelling to frontier outposts as needed. Department headquarters were in this building from June 1881 until 1886 when a new headquarters building was opened on donated land in near downtown St. Paul. Thereafter Building 67 was Fort Snelling's Post Headquarters. In 1883, a $1,000 contract installed the clock in the tower.

The building still looks now much as it did during World War II after the W.P.A. remodeled the interior. Civil War cannons once graced the front lawn and bronze commemorative bronze markers the west side of the building.

Headquarters, ca. late 1930s.

Post Headquarters, ca. 1938.

Trick horse Whiskey behind Headquarters, ca. 1925.

Military training was very limited. We did a lot of manual labor. There was lots of guard duty, particularly at the stables where the horses and mules were kept. Some of the fellows would sit on the mangers instead of walking the post and when they fell asleep, they'd fall off the manger and wake up. If the O.D. (Officer of the Day) would catch any of the guards asleep when he came to check the post, they would be given six months in the guardhouse. It happened to a buddy of mine. In those days, they didn't mind giving you the business. (J.K.)

Building 65 (C-4), Guard House

In 1891 a new prison, 60 x 85 feet and made of brick with a tile roof, was constructed to hold up to forty military prisoners. A 30 x 40 foot wing addition was built in 1912 and raised the capacity to 65 prisoners. This was the main guardhouse for the post, with smaller guardhouses in other areas such as the cantonment, the stables, gun sheds and the commissary. It only held men who were in for minor offenses. Prisoners were organized into guard work crews each day for tasks like washing windows, removing garbage and picking up trash. The Veterans' Administration Police and Fire Department staff used the building until the 1980s.

Guard House, ca. 1938.

Young George Leonard, Jr., was made an honorary member of the guard, ca. 1937.

Guard Duty, 1941.

Building 64 (C-10), Fire Station [Fire Station House]

The Fire Station as constructed in 1903.

The fire station replaced an earlier wooden structure in 1903 and was designed to store two ladder trucks and two hose reels. It measured 25 x 44 feet with a 23 x 42 foot wing, and had a tower on the rear for use as a lookout. Originally one story, the building had its tower removed when a second story was added probably just prior to World War II.

Behind this and other remaining permanent buildings there once stood wooden non-commissioned officer quarters, a chapel and schoolhouse, and various post, company and individual gardens.

Fire Station House, ca. 1938.

Building 63 (C-6), Non-commissioned Officers' Quarters [Quartermaster Shops]

The brick building to house shops for harness and saddle work among others was built in 1879–80. In 1930 the building was converted into quarters for eight non-commissioned officer families. Fort Snelling soldiers soon began calling it the "Incubator" for its reputed effect on the soldiers' wives living there. The historic structure, weakened for years from a leaking roof, collapsed in 2006 from snow load.

Non-commissioned Officers' Quarters, ca. 1938.

Building 57 (C-9), Barracks, Band

The two story 34 x 58 foot quarters with 12 x 20 foot wings was built in 1903 to house 28 musicians. As part of the Reconstruction General Hospital 29 complex just after World War I, it was used temporarily as an isolation hospital. The quarters were located close to headquarters areas because the band played for morning guard mounts and evening retreat ceremonies near the post flagpole. Early in 1942 the former 127th Field Artillery Band from Fort Ord moved in as the new Post Band. And at the end of World War II this building housed headquarters of the Military Intelligence Service Language School.

Bugle calls regulated the garrison's day, 1941.

Band Barracks, 1934.

Rear of band barracks, 2010.

Building 56 (G-4), Non-commissioned Officer Medical Department Quarters [Hospital Steward's Quarters]

As the post hospital was being completed, this 20 x 28 foot brick quarters with a 14-foot square wing was constructed in 1900 for the family of the hospital's principal non-commissioned officer.

Hospital Steward's Quarters as built, ca. 1905.

Non-commissioned Officer Medical Department Barracks, ca. 1938.

Building 54, Medical Detachment Barracks

The newest permanent military structure on the old post, this 39 x 155 foot brick building was constructed on a concrete foundation in 1939. It housed a medical detachment, part of post headquarters and made up of enlisted hospital orderlies and staff. The hospital staff served permanent party men, transient soldiers and summer trainees at Fort Snelling.

Medical Detachment Barracks, 1939.

Building 55 (G-3), Station Hospital
[Post Hospital]

The 45 x 54 foot post hospital with 36 beds and built in 1898, one of eight such permanent hospitals built with a $400,000 appropriation. Fort Snelling's new facility replaced an old wooden hospital which had been located about where the Mendota Bridge now meets the bluff. Two story wooden porches were originally along the front and two wings measuring 38 x 64 feet complemented the main building. More wings measuring 40 x 52 and 20 x 45 feet were added by 1908. At the end of World War I and into the 1920s it was known as the Surgical Pavilion of Reconstruction General Hospital Number 29 that encompassed much of the permanent post.

Even more additions were made in 1935 when capacity grew to 150 beds. A wooden "Victory Wing" was added to the rear in 1944 through donations from the Eastern Star fraternal order and was operated by the American Red Cross. Several temporary wooden ward buildings were located along the front on the opposite side of Taylor Avenue during World War II. The hospital's final use was as a U.S. Army Reserve hospital facility into the 1970s.

Temporary row wards on the parade ground opposite the Hospital.

Post Hospital, ca. 1920.

Nurses, General Hospital No. 29, ca. 1919.

Building 62 (G-6), Non-commissioned Officer's Quarters [Morgue]

In 1905 a 16.5 x 32 foot brick dead house or morgue was constructed just behind the hospital. Doubled in size to 34 x 32 feet in 1933 it continued as a morgue until 1938 when it was revamped into living quarters for a senior medical corps non commissioned officer and family.

The Dead House as constructed in 1905.

Non-commissioned Officers' Quarters, ca. 1938.

Building 53 (G-5), Gymnasium [Service Club]

The authorized strength of the army was raised from 25,000 to 60,000 men in 1902 in the wake of the Spanish American War and continued occupation of the Philippines. The next year an expenditure of $5.5 million was authorized for new construction and expansion at existing military posts. This appropriation funded gymnasiums and post exchanges for the first time, and soon an addition $3.5 million was authorized for post infrastructure. A new wave of improvements began at Fort Snelling.

The so called "Amusement Center for the Garrison" was constructed in 1903 as a massive 43 x 89.5 foot brick structure on a stone foundation. It was extensively remodeled in 1942–43 to a Service Club with a ballroom on second floor, a lounge, a reading room and pool tables on the main floor, and three bowling lanes and a branch PX in the basement. The Service Club hosted hundreds of dances and parties during World War II.

There wasn't an awful lot to do around Ft. Snelling in those days. We had a theater on the post and tickets were 35¢. There was also a service club where they used to hold dances or "G.I. belly rubs." Most of the guys went off-post to Minneapolis or St. Paul for entertainment. They could have a pretty good time for $3.00. To get uptown and back cost two streetcar tokens, which cost 10¢ apiece, or six for a buck. (J.K.)

The area removed by freeway construction in the late 1950s included the Post Theater built in 1931 and additional Officers' Quarters. Also near here was the site of the very important United States Indian Agency built in 1820 by the army and managed by Indian Agent Lawrence Taliaferro.

Fire drill outside the Gymnasium, 1930s.

Army band marches past the Gymnasium, 1918.

Basketball game in the Gymnasium, 1937.

Fort Snelling is currently under administration of a variety of agencies. Most of the land southeast of Bloomington road was ceded to the State of Minnesota in the 1960s and 1970s. The Minnesota Historical Society manages the old Lower Post area for historical monument purposes. The fully restored/reconstructed frontier fortress is open for tours during the summer months. The parade grounds and other areas adjacent to Bloomington Road, also state property, are leased to the Minneapolis Parks and Recreation Department. The buildings along Taylor Avenue are under control of the Department of Natural Resources. Northwest of Bloomington Road the Veterans Administration and the General Services Administration administer property still under federal ownership.

Newly arrived M.I.S.L.S. student at Reception Center Barracks

The Reception Center, Officers' Club, Ranges, and National Cemetery

Reached via the Post Road and the 34th Avenue exits off Minnesota Highway 5, west of the Twin Cities International Airport.

Fort Snelling was a relatively small post of only 1,521 acres yet numbered over 400 structures by 1945. Typical garrison and transient troop populations were between 3,000 and 5,000 during the war years. The area north of the highway where airport hangers and runway now stand was the site of the Recruit Reception Station with its over 200 wooden barracks—known as "dog houses" or 'The Turkey Farm"—and later concrete block mess halls, latrines, guard houses and training buildings. East of this complex was the Old Post Cemetery used from the 1880s until 1938.

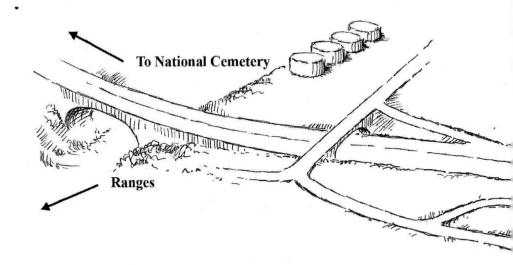

North of the highway on the west, and in the ravine behind the large white fuel tanks along Post Road, were machine gun and pistol ranges. Beyond were maneuver areas with World War I style trenches and dugouts. During the early 19th century this ravine running down to the Minnesota River was known as "Land's End" and was the site of a trading post operated by the Columbia Fur Company. During World War II and earlier Fort Snelling's rifle ranges were located in this area.

Further west and reached from the 34th Avenue exit is the Fort Snelling National Cemetery laid out in 1938 and now containing burials dating back to Fort Snelling's founding in 1819.

I got my greetings from the U.S. Army. They asked if I wouldn't be so kind as to join them. They were still having trouble with Hitler and they thought I could probably make a difference. I got orders to report to Ft. Snelling for induction around the 15th of December, 1943. Owing to the fact that most of us drafted in 1943 were around 30 years of age, married, and established in careers, there were a high percentage of attorneys, policemen, FBI agents, state troopers in our cadre. In spite of all the hassle, these fellows were real morale builders and there was seldom a dull moment. (J.K.)

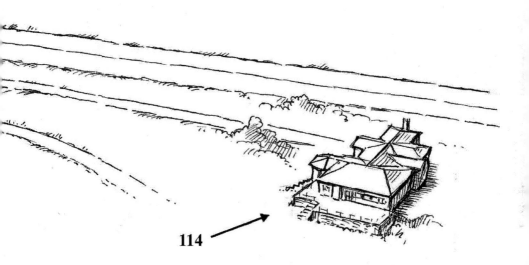

114

Drawing not to scale

We are quartered in the War Department Personnel Headquarters Building and there are two WACs to a nice bedroom. We have a nice dayroom, bath and shower. There are nine WACs here – the first white WACs ever to be stationed at Snelling. We eat at the Officers' Mess. Headquarters Company Col. Curtis, Lt. Hart (WAC): These two have done everything to make our army home happy and comfortable. (Sgt. Marian Winter, July 1945)

Reception Center Headquarters and Barracks, ca. 1943.

Arriving at Fort Snelling, we found it filled with large new wooden barracks and offices. We were given steel bunks on the second floor of a barracks. Here we encountered a few self-important Privates First Class and Corporals. There were also a considerable number of older non-commissioned officers who had served in WWI. They were factual and told us not to listen to the tales of the young puppies. Next, we were scattered into long lines of naked men, holding our papers, for medical exam. Soon we were given intelligence quotient exams, and many different medical exams for general health and vision . . . Next, we were interviewed by psychologists. Then, there were more special interviews with young men who had many general reference books. They would quiz us for our knowledge on auto mechanics and radio theory, etc., and refer to their books for questions to test our knowledge. (Alan Woolworth, inducted February 1943.)

Bud Nakasone gathers coal to feed his hutment stove, 1945.

The old Cantonment in 1936.

A 1940 view showing new Barracks.

Building 114 (B-10), Officers' Country Club [Officers' Club]

The present Fort Snelling Officers' Club was opened in 1934 replacing a cramped club that operated out of the Bachelor Officers' Quarters. The new club even featured its own three lane bowling alley in the basement. Enlisted men staffed the facility and parked cars. On the grounds was a swimming pool for officers and their families, picnic grounds, and the first holes of a golf course with its own clubhouse. A variety of recreational activities were organized here including mounted foxhunts, weekly dances in the ballroom, and summer poolside barbeques. Recently renovated, the Club is currently operated by the U.S. Air Force Reserve to serve military officers, retirees and civilians. The interior still features rustic wood and stonework fabricated by skilled C.C.C. Craftsmen.

I remember the officers' club was in the process of being built and I was put in charge of a squad of C.C.C. boys. We had a wagon and a team of mules with which we hauled flat rocks up from the river bottom for some of the stone work being done at the club. We'd get the wagon loaded up and the mules couldn't get the wagon up the steep embankment. At this point, we all had to jump off the wagon and push. (J.K.)

Workers quarry stone for the new Officers' Club, ca. 1934.

Officers' Country Club, 1939.

Jacob Klotzbeacher on leave with family, 1944.

Officers' wives at the club, 1936.

Clubroom later occupied by Officers' Club bar, ca. 1940.

Bowling alley in basement of the club, ca. 1940.

Stephen Osman

managed Historic Fort Snelling for over three decades, and was the last resident of the Officers' Quarters (Building 2) at the post. While an Army Reservist he drilled in the old Barracks (Building 103). It was there in the early 1970s that he first met then Colonel Bud Nakasone and enjoyed chatting with then First Sergeant Jacob Klotzbeacher. The author was assisted by Todd Hintz, an amateur historian who produces WWII history displays and serves on the Friends of Fort Snelling board. Images were taken and/or edited by Matt Flueger, a classically trained fine arts photographer who has documented surviving elements of Fort Snelling for several years.

This book is brought to you by volunteers of

The Friends of Fort Snelling

Our Purpose

To Preserve
- The natural and historical resources of the unique area where the Minnesota and Mississippi rivers converge and peoples have been meeting for centuries.

To Promote
- Recreational opportunities in the metropolitan Twin Cites' only state park;
- Educational opportunities using Fort Snelling's nationally-significant historical resources;
- Increased citizen support for continuing development of these public sites.

To Assist
- Fort Snelling sites staffs with acquisition of resources to maintain and improve programs and amenities;
- The professional staffs of the sites with educational and recreational programs.

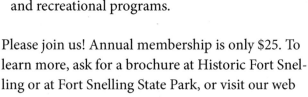

Please join us! Annual membership is only $25. To learn more, ask for a brochure at Historic Fort Snelling or at Fort Snelling State Park, or visit our web site: www.fortsnelling.org